GOD'S STORY

Through...

GOD'S

LIGHT

GOD'S STORY
Through...
GOD'S LIGHT

Designing, Restoring, Protecting and Insulating your church stained glass heritage...

A Series of Articles
By Dr. Gary M. Gray, FCBA
Stained Glass Consultant

iUniverse, Inc.
New York Lincoln Shanghai

God's Story Through...God's Light
Designing, Restoring, Protecting and Insulating
your church stained glass heritage...

iUniverse books may be ordered through booksellers or by contacting:

iUniverse
2021 Pine Lake Road, Suite 100
Lincoln, NE 68512
www.iuniverse.com
1-800-Authors (1-800-288-4677)

ISBN-13: 978-0-595-40374-5 (pbk)
ISBN-13: 978-0-595-84749-5 (ebk)
ISBN-10: 0-595-40374-3 (pbk)
ISBN-10: 0-595-84749-8 (ebk)

Printed in the United States of America

Dedicated to Tom Lee and Lyle Harlos

Contents

Large Willet Stained Glass window at St. Paul United Methodist Church, Louisville, Kentucky

INTRODUCTION

Throughout America there is a thirst for information about stained glass. One of the truly delightful joys of my life has been talking to ministers, church administrators, facilities managers, but most of all laypersons, about their own local church stained glass.

When I entered the stained glass field in 1984, I was primarily known as a churchman. I had been to seminary and I specialized in understanding church dynamics. When it came to stained glass, I was as awed as anyone.

Two thousand visits to local churches to inspect their stained glass heritage has changed me a bit. Yet I still get the thrill of seeing a sanctuary for the first time…to gaze upon incredibly beautiful and intricate portrayals of biblical scenes…and to ascertain just what message that church was trying to convey with their theme and artistry. I've learned congregational members are extremely proud of God's message their windows tell through God's light.

Several years ago a national church magazine asked me to write an article about stained glass, others then followed. I've found it is impossible to tell the entire story of stained glass in an article…at least the story that I have been involved with…stained glass design, restoration, protection, and insulation. Thus with each article another key element was added.

GOD'S STORY THROUGH GOD'S LIGHT, quite simply, is a booklet made up of a series of articles, each focusing on stained glass from a different perspective. The reader will find the various articles overlap somewhat, as each article was a read unto itself. I decided to leave it that way, as I anticipate the reader focusing on the stained glass needs of specific articles.

Regardless, stained glass is an ancient, kinetic art that has been inspiring the masses for 900 years. When stained glass is first created, it requires considerable thought and planning to combine the theme, artistic style, colors, and shape into an artistic masterpiece that will speak to individuals each time it is gazed upon, whatever decade that may be. At the same time, church building and grounds committees need to be aware of the ongoing needs of leaded stained glass.

Stained glass, as will be mentioned repeatedly in the upcoming articles, is usually the most central source of a congregation's message (within the building itself). Therefore, create with great care, then serve as good stewards of your heritage by utilizing the time-honored steps of conserving stained glass for future generations.

Gary M. Gray

Barber Memorial Window, "Angel and Child" by Tiffany Studios, at First United Methodist Church, Colorado Springs, Colorado. Using thick flowing and rippled glass for the robes in biblical scenes, the Tiffany family of artistry (along with the similar windows of John LaFarge), represents the best in American stained glass.

Chapter I

THE STAINED GLASS STORY

Many times I have entered a church just to take a peek inside, and in nearly every case, my eyes were immediately drawn to the stained-glass windows. If the architecture had been distinctive enough to create curiosity, almost assuredly I could say that the congregation had taken great pains to tell God's story through a festival of color and light. Even though the pulpit or the altar might be exceedingly beautiful and symbolically meaningful, it was the stained glass pictorials, symbols and patterns that captured my attention and thoughts.

Church leaders have long known the spiritual qualities of this unique medium; actually a fusion of nature and art. Since the 11th century, churches have turned Bible stories into a visual drama, offering worshippers a "slide show" that held God's story up to the light.

Thus, stained glass has had an impact on this world for nearly 900 years. That impact has been powerful, magnificent and unique, while telling the biblical story. Better than any other form of communication, stained glass takes advantage of God's light to add brilliance to the storyteller's art.

Stained glass emerged primarily as an European art form. Artists and craftsmen could spend lifetimes designing, firing, and fabricating a cathedral's leaded glass masterpieces. Most of America's greatest stained glass, during the nineteenth century, was made in Germany and Britain, or some came from France and Italy. Typical of these windows were biblical scenes exquisite in detail and color. The painted faces and hands were remarkably lifelike. By walking slowly from window-to-window, one could picture, for example, the Nativity scene; the young Jesus at the temple; His baptism, ministry, trial, crucifixion, resurrection and ascension. Thus, the stained glass visually told the Christian message to the illiterate masses.

Willet window (circa 1950s) at Northern Oklahoma College, Enid, Oklahoma. Willet windows are known to use blues and reds as the dominate colors, and usually have multiple pictorial scenes.

Although excellent examples of stained glass masterpieces existed in the United States prior, its greatest surge was the period of 1880-1917. Primarily, these windows were designed by German, English, French and Italian artists creating detailed pictorial biblical scenes. Many of these artists eventually moved to America and continued their artistic trade for American churches and synagogues.

At the turn of the twentieth century, American stained glass briefly became the world's finest when Louis Comfort Tiffany took the art to new heights. Eccentric, brilliant, and wealthy, Tiffany created new forms for molding thick rippled glass using strikingly beautiful pastel colors. Unconcerned about profit, Tiffany sought to create the ultimate stained glass masterpiece; a goal he achieved in church after church.

American stained glass quality remained high during the thirties and forties with the emergence of such studios as Connick, Willet, Payne and Lamb. By the half-century mark, however, an inferior product predominated. In many respects this was due to the death or retirement of the founding artists of those studios, a national de-emphasis on art and craftsmanship, and the church's desires for quick property expansion rather than lasting inspiration.

Although the industry remains substantially below the standards of Tiffany, Connick, Willet and other artists of the early 1900s, a slow resurgence of quality and care has taken place since the 1980s. Much of the resurgence has been in faceted glass (a thick brilliantly colored glass fastened with epoxy). Even leaded glass, in some disfavor in recent decades, shows a healthy comeback.

Why Stained Glass?

What are the reasons for this renewal of interest? It seems that stained glass meets some human desires and needs that are not otherwise fulfilled:

The Story—No other form of art so perfectly blends God's great gift of light with the impact of the visualized biblical story. The stained glass scenes are often one's earliest remembrance of a church experience. Long before a child is able to absorb the verbal message, he or she can contemplate the conceptual one told visually through stained glass.

Pre-World War I Catholic windows, like this one at St. Joseph's Catholic Parish in Hays, Kansas, were highly detailed and told key portions of the scriptures. Catholics traditionally protected their stained glass at the time of installation. Having never experienced the elements, vandalism, or robbery, these windows have remained in relatively excellent condition despite having been created one hundred years ago.

Tradition and Heritage—So powerful is the relationship between the stained glass window and the church, it is difficult to imagine one without the other. Recent decades have seen a valid emphasis on the church ministry rather than the church building, but the longing to have inspirational windows has helped church leaders view stained glass as a tangible ministry of its own…one that is timeless. An increasing number of new sanctuaries are being built not only for current space, but in addition, as a heritage for future generations.

Inspirational Art—A couple of decades ago a fifteen square foot Tiffany window was advertised for $60,000—a staggering $4,000 per square foot. Although such prices are a rarity, European and American pictorial stained glass has replacement values approaching $500 to $900 per square foot. Consistently, therefore, it is the church's stained glass windows that are the greatest pieces of art. When beautiful and inspirational stained glass art does exist, the church leaders invariably gather volunteers to lead guests on informational tours of the windows. It is the church window that often leaves the most lasting impression of a church building. If they have inspired, or told the biblical story, the investment has become fruitful.

Perpetuation—To be remembered past one's lifetime is a basic human need. Probably 50% or more of stained glass windows have been given in remembrance of a loved one. Since stained glass can be periodically restored (and protected and insulated from the elements), the window and the name can endure far into the future.

It is not surprising that a stained glass revival is again sweeping America. Artistic voids of these last few decades are being filled with light, brilliance and beauty. As America is returning to the scriptures in record numbers, stained glass is being used to help tell the story. Likewise, as America returns to old fashioned craftsmanship, so too are stained glass studios gathering the world's great artists and craftsmen to design and fabricate modern masterpieces, and to perform careful restoration, protection and insulation of our valuable heritage. It is an exciting time for stained glass, for the church, and for Christianity.

University Baptist Church in Ft. Worth, Texas

Chapter II

BUILDING STAINED GLASS INTO YOUR FUTURE

I have one of the most wonderful jobs in the world. Each year I inspect some of the most beautiful and inspirational stained glass in the United States. Even though I possibly visit 100 church buildings a year, I almost always gasp and follow that with a "wow." There is simply something about stained glass that each congregation should experience.

It is the reaction of the lay committee that meets with me that may be the most telling. Invariably, there is a pride in the stained glass; a pride that is not found in any other portion of the building. As we pass from one window to the next, the layperson often talks about the symbolism or scene. Each one has its own story, and each one has spoken over the years to different congregants in different ways.

Important Trends

Two trends are taking place in new church construction today that some say will lead to the demise of stained glass.

First, because of such a strong emphasis on new forms of media and music, the "new" sanctuary is often being built to be totally dark inside, allowing for lighting, sound, and visual systems to be flexible for all forms of contemporary worship. Often committees forget that stained glass was God's original slide show; it allowed God's light to penetrate the beautifully colored or painted/fired glass to tell His story.

Second, there is a tendency toward "economy." "Stained glass would be nice," one committee person told me, "but we don't have the money."

Compelling Reasons

Look at these compelling reasons to include stained glass in your new construction plans:

Inspiration*:* One only needs to look at the face of a child gazing upon stained glass to appreciate its value…which is priceless. Many a lay leader has told me it was the stained glass that got them through sermons when they were children…and sometimes even as an adult.

Imagine a series of windows on the north wall of your new building. It has scenes of Jesus' life from his birth, baptism, ministry, last supper, trial, crucifixion, resurrection, and ascension. On the south wall is the story of God's promise to his "chosen people" from Adam and Eve, Noah, Abraham, Isaac, Jacob, Joseph, Moses, David and the prophets." As the congregation exits to the east, there is the story of the new church at Pentecost, and the ministries of Peter and Paul as Christianity is taken into the world. The window above the baptistery is a quiet, yet majestic image of…Imagine that…

Heritage*:* While it is fine to build the church building for today, one must also build for the future, which means you provide something for your congregation upon which a heritage is founded.

One of the strongest trends in new church construction is from long established churches.…the one thing congregants want moved to the new site is the stained glass. Stained glass has power that should not be underestimated. The fancy equipment the church is using now will soon be antiquated; stained glass never will.

Fund Raising: Nothing in the life of a church raises money easier than does stained glass (with the possible exception of a pipe organ). Recently, I presented a design for a fabulous stained glass window for a large chapel. Its cost? $75,000. Although the committee loved the design and could see the value of the window for the chapel, it was the money that almost overwhelmed them. I insisted that they take the design to just one or two people for funding. Apparently, the committee did not have to speak to the second person. A check for the entire amount was written the day of the first presentation.

Stained glass draws an unbelievable amount of money from sources a congregation would not often touch. Look at the benefits: that chapel has a masterpiece that presents a biblical message, and the family involved receives great satisfaction of knowing they have left their congregation with something inspirational for decades (probably centuries).

Countering the Arguments

Exponents of light and beauty only need to counter the arguments. Try these…

Do Not Close Out God's light: While designing a new church building to be in complete darkness might have its merits for some purposes or for the style of the current minister. We all know trends and ministers change. There are many effective ways to have the brilliance of light streaming through stained glass, and then simply push a button to have shades covering the glass for the few moments a visual presentation needs darkness.

There is just something wrong with a building created for darkness and artificial light. Think about it!

If the pastor is insistent upon darkness, there are other ways of providing the stained glass for the congregation. What about a huge entryway "creation" image as the people enter and depart worship?

What about stained glass at the end of walkways in the educational buildings, or a mixture of glass and light along the top of the fellowship hall?

Chief Fund Raiser: If you are among those on the building committee who still believes your congregation cannot afford stained glass, you are most likely wrong.

…Or the argument goes like this:

> *"Sure we have several who would pay for the stained glass but we need those same people to pay for the rest of the building. There's not very much pizzazz in building a roof or providing a restroom."*

In this case they are right!!

This faceted window at Moody Memorial United Methodist in Galveston, Texas was created by Gabriel Loire (1904-1996). At the time of his death, Loire was "Artist-in-Residence" at Chartres Cathedral, Chartres, France.

So, here is the solution. Let's say you have met with a stained glass designer who has provided you a $20,000 design for the altar area. Don't ask someone to give $20,000 for the window, ask for $100,000! Now I am not for the moment suggesting dishonesty here; quite the opposite.

I suggest you tell some of your key donors of church:

> *We have seven stained glass windows proposed for the new sanctuary. We would like for your family to take on the Altar window. If you do so, we would welcome you placing a nameplate in the window in memory of your*

beloved mother who passed last year. We are suggesting $100,000 as one of the lead gifts for the church building fund. That amount not only will cover the actual costs of the window but go a long way to help us reach our over-all goal. Would you like the altar window or the one in the chapel?

To be remembered past one's lifetime is a basic human need. Probably 50% or more of stained glass windows have been given in remembrance of a loved one. Since stained glass can be periodically restored (and protected and insulated from the elements), the window and the name can endure far into the future. Perpetuation needs generate enormous fund-raising powers. If appropriate, utilize those needs for God's building.

Thus, do not construct a building in darkness; instead, build one that tells the story of God's handiwork that a worshipper can gaze upon throughout his or her life's Christian journey.

Do not think small and economical, but rather dream dreams and imagine the image of the Bible shining through the walls, and know that you can fund those images far easier than to not have them at all.

Build stained glass into your future.

The Baylor Baptist Hospital chapel window (Plano, Texas),
designed by Russell Joy for Stained Glass by Shenandoah

Chapter III

THE INGREDIENTS
OF STAINED GLASS

Your congregation has just voted to build a new sanctuary. One of the most important items, several members say, is to have beautiful stained glass—whatever that means. As the chairperson of the new stained-glass subcommittee, you are to lead the process of design selection. Your committee's decision not only will impact those who worship there in the sanctuary's first few years but quite possibly worshippers for centuries to come.

Many factors can influence the final decision. The input from the architect or a liturgical consultant is usually valuable. Artistic persons from the congregation can be helpful. In the end, however, you learn that creating the right stained-glass windows for the sanctuary requires careful attention to five critical ingredients.

Theme

Choosing the theme or subject of a stained-glass design is the central ingredient of your decision. The original stained glass from the twelfth and thirteenth centuries was created to tell the biblical story to the uneducated masses. Biblical scenes continue to dominate the themes chosen in the 21st century. Still, some stained-glass committees have shown remarkable creativity in their use of biblical themes. Rather than automatically choosing obvious scenes—Jesus knocking at the door, for example, or the Good Shepherd—congregations can select biblical themes unique to them and their message.

The decision made by the Mount Olivet congregation serves as a good illustration. Since Mount Olivet is another name for the Mount of Olives, the stained-glass committee searched the scriptures for references related to the Mount of Olives. The one nearly everyone knew was Christ's prayer in the Garden of Gethsemane. That meant the betrayal of Jesus also took place on the Mount. Further research,

Connick Associates (circa 1960) at St. Mark's Episcopal Church, Cheyenne, Wyoming. Connick of Boston was one of America's greatest stained glass compani

Modern style windows at Montview Presbyterian Church, Denver, Colorado

however, revealed less-known connections: the triumphal entry began on Mount Olivet; Jesus' ascension into heaven took place on its slopes; and many other biblical applications can be found for the olive and the olive tree. The Mount Olivet congregation found a biblical theme that tied in with their own name, providing the stained-glass designer with many unique ideas.

Biblical themes, however, are not the only choice for a committee. Historical, regional, and denominational themes have also been popular and appropriate. Even the most abstract windows can display themes such as creation or a sunrise.

Design Style

The first great heyday of American stained glass was between 1890 and 1917, when America built massive naves with traditional pictorial stained glass, most of it painted and fired. These were designed and fabricated by German, English, French and Italian artists primarily, many of whom had immigrated to America near the turn of the century. Strictly American stained glass used ordered Gothic, Roman and rectangular designs with a heavy use of round glass "jewels."

Today the excessive costs of painted and fired pictorial glass, plus the changing tastes of consumers, have made the traditional window less popular. And though modern artists may use pictorials or medallions to focus their theme, they may also use simple backgrounds in traditional, contemporary, or abstract form for the remaining space. Fortunately, for those who do desire the traditional biblical pictorial scene, there are a few modern artists who can paint "flesh" in the same style and manner as those great European and American artists of a century ago. Other options available to stained-glass committees include leaded stained glass and faceted glass (thick one-inch, colored glass cemented with epoxy).

Shape

A critical element of your design plan is the shape of the windows. This should be considered early in the process so that shape, where possible, is influenced by the theme and design style, rather than the other way around. A designer can reinforce the theme of the windows through their shape to utilize the majesty of stained glass in concert with surrounding architecture.

*One hundred plus year old American style windows at All Souls Unitarian
Universalist Church, Colorado Springs, Colorado. Notice the use of
round "jewels" in this window. This is a characteristic of American stained glass
which began to disappear about 1900 (almost totally by 1910).
Modern stained glass companies have begun to feature the "jewel" again.*

A full wall of stained glass, for example, evokes a decidedly different feeling for the worshiper than does a series of Gothic or circular windows. Involve the architect early in discussion with the stained-glass committee to ensure that the chosen window shape fits the overall building design. Other factors—size, number, and placement—should also be considered initially.

Color

Unlike the colors selected for carpeting, pew cushions, and choir robes, the hues chosen for the stained-glass windows cannot be readily changed. The colors in your windows will affect the congregation for as long as that sanctuary is used. Since colors affect our emotions—some evoke peace, others strength and power—select your colors carefully. *Rule of thumb: Stick with more basic colors and avoid trendy ones. Also be careful about the depth of colors. Too little color can cause a glare problem; too much color depth can make the sanctuary dark and dreary.*

Budget

What happens when your committee's aesthetic tastes call for a $520-per-square foot design while your budget has allotted only $120? Compromise will likely be necessary, requiring a simpler design or smaller windows along with an increase in budget. However, many churches have found that funding stained-glass windows is easier than raising funds for most other church items. People respond readily to the idea of inspiring stained-glass windows and often give toward windows as a memorial to a loved one. *Suggestion: Determine your budget early in the discussion so the designer can work within certain constraints and create a design only as intricate as available funds allow.*

The creation of new stained glass can be a wonderful adventure, especially if your committee has an early understanding about the five elements of a good stained-glass decision. Your first discussions should center on the themes of the windows—bringing focus to the committee early in the process. The remaining ingredients of design style, shape, color, and budget can then round out the clear guidance your design artist needs to do the job. This process will assure you of acquiring a unique stained-glass design with a specific message for your congregation and building.

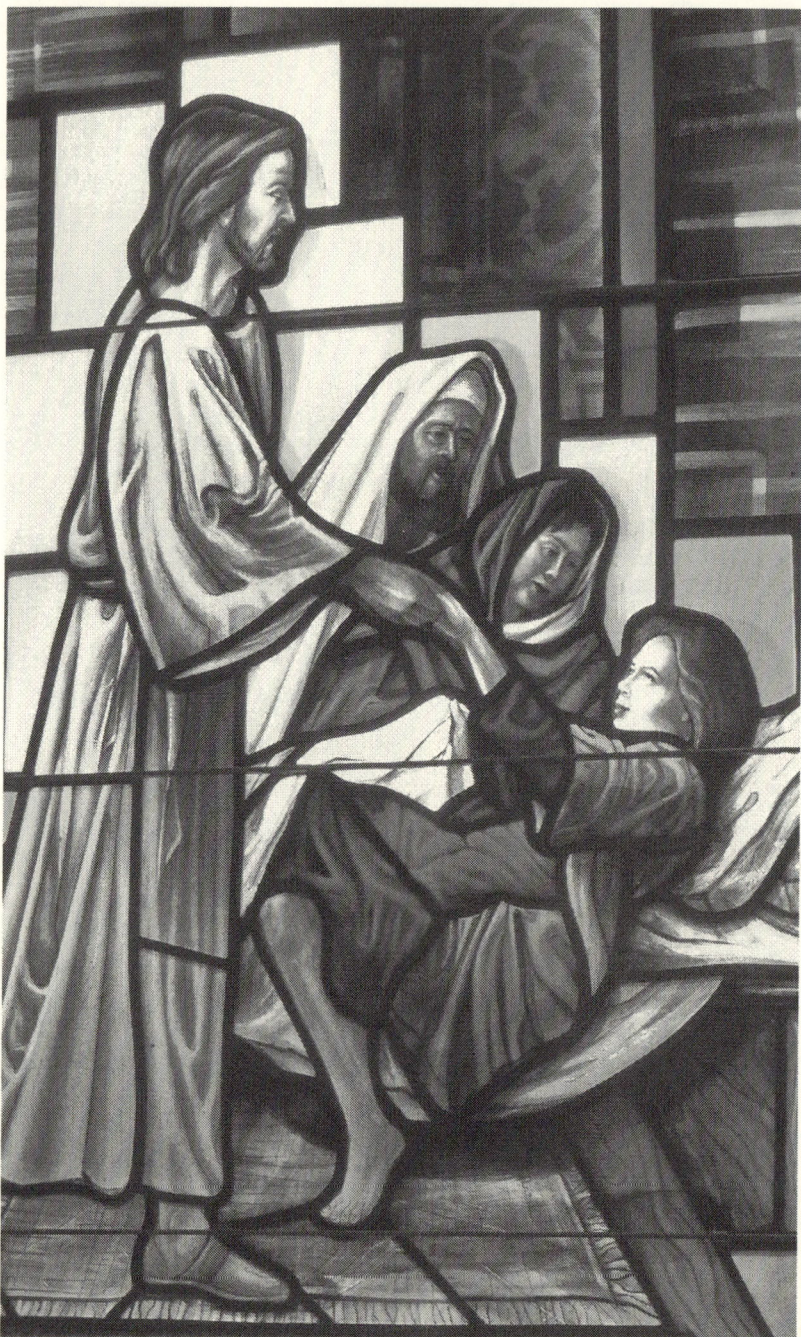

Baylor Baptist Hospital Chapel in Plano, Texas.
Designed by Russell Joy for Stained Glass by Shenandoah.

Chapter IV

HOW A STAINED
GLASS WINDOW IS MADE

Stained glass is a hand craft, and is practiced in America today in virtually the same manner as it was in the Middle Ages. Modern technique is comparable to that of the twelfth and thirteenth centuries in Europe, although some of the tools—notably the glass cutter and the soldering iron—have been improved for rapid and more skillful handling.

The steps in the production of stained glass windows are briefly as follows:

The making of the *design* comes first. It is usually a small-scale study of the window, intended to convey an impression of the color and light of the full-sized window.

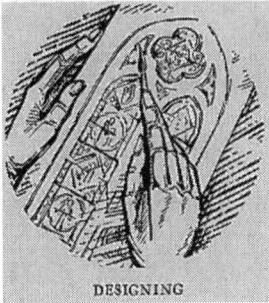
DESIGNING

After the design has been approved by the donor, committee, clergy, or others interested, the craftsman takes measurements or templates of the actual window openings. The template is a pattern, usually on paper or cardboard, of the actual size of the spaces to be filled with glass.

A full-sized drawing called the *cartoon* is next prepared, generally in black and white. The suggestions of the first sketch are developed further in the cartoon.

From the cartoon, the *cutline* and *pattern* drawings are made. The modern cutline drawing is a careful, exact tracing of the leadlines of the cartoon on heavy paper. The leadlines are the outlines of the shapes for patterns from which the glass is to be cut. This draw-

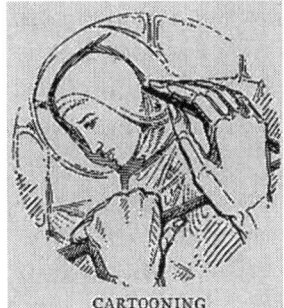
CARTOONING

ing serves as guide or reference for the subsequent placing and binding with lead of the many pieces of glass.

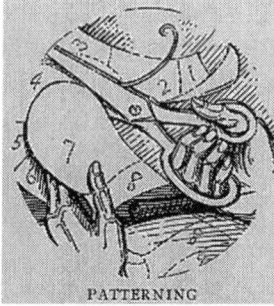

PATTERNING

The pattern-drawing, usually on heavy paper, is a carbon copy of the cutline drawing. It is cut along the black or lead lines with double-bladed scissors or knife which, as it passes through the middle of the black lines, simultaneously cuts away a narrow strip of paper, thus allowing sufficient space between segments of glass for the core of the grooved lead. This core is the supporting wall between the upper and lower flanges of the lead, which is something like a miniature girder or like the letter H lying on its side.

The medieval craftsman had no preliminary sketch, unless it was an illumination on parchment; nor had he paper patterns. His first step was to smooth a wooden slab twice the size of a window panel. On this he scraped chalk, sprinkled it with water, and spread the paste around until the entire board was covered. He measured off the size of the panel on half the board, and carefully drew such figures as he desired, going over the lines with red or black, perhaps with the self-same colors used by the monks in the scriptorium for illuminating manuscripts.

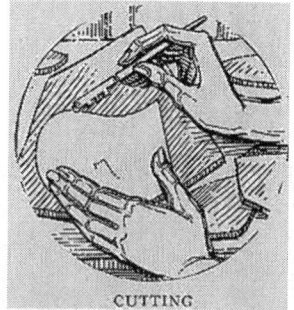

CUTTING

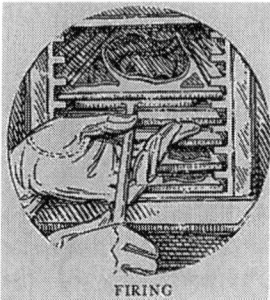

FIRING

The drawing served not only as cartoon, but as cutline and pattern, and later for tracing significant form.

The glass is then selected from the large stock always kept on hand. The glass cutter places the pattern on a piece of the desired color, and with a diamond or steel wheel cuts the glass to the shape of the pattern.

In the Middle Ages the glass was cut with a tool which was nothing more than a sharply pointed rod of iron, heated to a high temperature. The red hot point was drawn along the moistened surface of the glass placed over the chalked cartoon, and the glass snapped apart. The fracture was not very accurate and the rough piece had to be chipped or grozed down to the exact shape with the help of hooked tools called grozing irons.

After the glass has all been cut, the *painter* takes over. He paints on each piece of glass, with special vitrifiable paint, the main outlines of the cartoon. Further patterning is applied in halftone mats to control the light and bring all the colors into closer harmony.

Much of this painting is done while the glass is up in the light, held in place on a plate glass easel by means of beeswax. In this way the painter approximates the conditions in which the window will eventually be seen. These painted pieces are *fired* in the kiln at least once and perhaps several times to fuse the paint and glass.

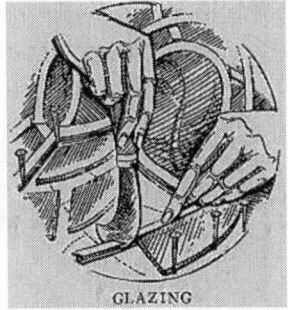

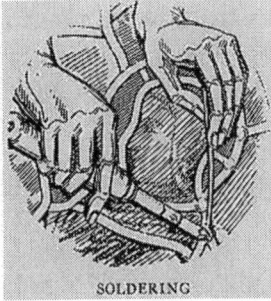

GLAZING

The glass is now ready for the *glazier*. The cutline drawing is spread on the glazier's bench and laths are nailed down along two edges of the drawing to form a right angle. Long strips of wide lead are placed along the inside of the laths. The piece of glass belonging in the angle is fitted into the grooved lead. A strip of narrow lead is fitted around the exposed edge or edges and the next required segment slipped into the groove on the other side of the narrow lead. This is continued until each piece has been inserted into the leads in its

SOLDERING

proper place according to the outline drawing beneath. The many joints formed by the leading are *soldered*; and the entire window is *cemented* on both sides to make it firm and water-tight. The window is made in sections of a size convenient for one man to handle.

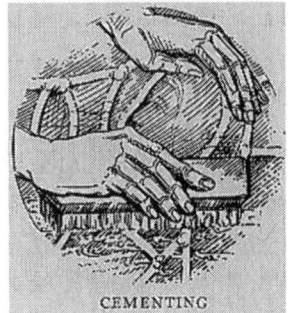

After the completed window has been thoroughly inspected in the light, the sections are packed and shipped to their destination where they are installed and secured with reinforcing bars.

CEMENTING

Planning for Windows

The inexperienced may find themselves at a loss to know just how to go about the procurement of stained glass.

If the structure in which a window or group of windows is to be placed is a new one, the services of the architect may be enlisted. Even if the building is not new, the architect may still be available and he will be interested in the enrichment of his creation. His advice should be valued, and he may refer his client to other authorities familiar with stained glass.

There are a number of good books on the subject which can be found in most public libraries.

One may go to see windows in the neighborhood that are recommended by capable authorities. Then write or call on one of the designers whose work is liked, giving him as much information as possible. The style of architecture of the structure is of first importance. The designer wants to know the size and shape of the windows; that is, the measurements of the actual glass or daylight openings, and whether the tops are rectangular, round, Gothic arched or indented with cusps or points. He will be interested in the direction of the light they receive,—north, south, east or west,—and whether neighboring trees or buildings obstruct the light stream. The height of the windows from the floor, their position in the building, and their relation to any windows that may be nearby, are also matters that will concern him.

This chapter was taken from "The Story of Stained Glass," prepared and sponsored by the Stained Glass Association of America.

A portion of the First United Methodist Church dome in Gulfport, Mississippi

Chapter V

APPRECIATING STAINED GLASS

I made two visits to Gulfport, Mississippi in 2005. The first was in August after two minor hurricanes had brushed the community. My visit was to inspect the stained glass and the protective covering at First United Methodist Church. I had been there in 1986 to arrange for the stained glass to be repaired and a new protective covering (3/16" LEXAN XL sheets) installed.

I had almost forgotten FUMC's enormous dome. It has magnificent and charming biblical scenes prepared in intricate detail. I reclined on a pew for a few moments just to view its beauty and message. In a trustees' meeting that evening, I reported the dome measured 1202 square feet and had a replacement value of approximately $781,300.

Ironically I was invited to stay and attend a dinner with the new mayor of Gulfport, Brent Warr, who outlined his long-range plans for Gulfport. Three weeks later I was horrified as news came of Hurricane Katrina blasting Gulfport.

When I returned in December 2005 to survey the post-Katrina damage, I found most everything in downtown Gulfport devastated. The Baptist Church was left a shell of itself with all its stained glass completely destroyed. Because of the storm surge, all the first floor windows at the Presbyterian and Episcopal churches were but skeletons.

The stained glass windows at First Christian were saved by an excellent installation of protective covering. Fortunately so were those sanctuary windows at First United Methodist…and the dome made it too!!!

Unfortunately for the United Methodists, the stained glass in the educational building was not well protected, and a considerable amount of moderately valuable glass was either seriously damaged or obliterated.

This little angel statue is the only item undamaged at St. Peter's By the Sea Episcopal, Gulfport. It seems to still be trying to push the storm away.

It should now be obvious that churches everywhere along our coasts need to be concerned with the disaster a hurricane can wreak. But damage can occur anywhere, anytime. The most common culprit is large hail, another is fire, a third vandalism, and sometimes there is burglary. Beautiful, incredibly valuable, totally irreplaceable windows are destroyed in an instant.

Take for example First United Methodist Church and St. Joseph Co-Cathedral in Oklahoma City. Both parishes' sanctuaries were next door to the Murrah Federal Building on April 19, 1995 when it was bombed. The stained glass facing the Murrah Building in both churches was obliterated.

The glass could be found, but it was in pieces less that one-half inch in diameter. The remnant pieces were so small there was no hope for duplication, not even for an adequate photographic history. No church could have been prepared for such an evil assault.

So what is a congregation to do? There are four important steps.

Photographic library: Arrange for a professional photographer to systematically make a thorough and detailed series of photographs of each stained glass window, no matter how insignificant or valuable. Make several copies of this inventory, keeping several in safe keeping elsewhere (one copy should be in the church's safe deposit box). Other copies should be in storage within the computers of local church members. Then if fire, hail, winds, vandalism, or robbery strikes, a photographic record is available so the stained glass windows can be replicated (if possible and/or desired).

Professional Appraisal: *So what are our windows worth?* I've heard church after church member simply say: *"we've been told our windows are priceless."* It's caused me to almost choke when I find a basic collection of leaded colored glass with a simple medallion. Priceless indeed!!! Yet most pictorial stained glass created prior to 1955 is valuable, some of it "priceless."

If the windows were made by Connick, Lamb, Payne, or Willet prior to 1955, then the windows are extremely valuable. Replacement of these windows (and it increases with age and amount/detail of the art work) is often as high as $500-$900 a square foot.

Hurricane Katrina's storm surge destroyed First Presbyterian Church, Gulfport. These two flags, one Christian, the other American, stood guard at the devastated entrance.

If the windows are Franz Meyer or F. X. Zettler windows from Munich, Germany pre 1917, the replacement values are the same or possibly even higher (those from the 1885-1910 eras are spectacular). If they are John LaFarge or Louis Comfort Tiffany windows (especially if they were signed personally by the artists), then yes, they are priceless.

Today, the masterpieces in stained glass art are made (predominately) by member companies of the Stained Glass Association of America. Some of their work is commissioned at prices exceeding $1,000 per square foot. Most, of course, are not at that level, but the "great" expressions of biblical art are expensive. If disaster hits a recent window, there is a strong likelihood that records exist at the studio to allow a relatively easy replication, but time is always an enemy. Eventually all stained glass studios cease to exist, and records are lost.

Since the word "priceless" is irrelevant in case of disaster, it is important to know what the windows are worth, and when possible, a history of each window is helpful. Therefore, a professional stained glass appraisal is critical, one that lists all the windows individually, and provides a dollar replacement value on each along with other valuable histories and observations.

Stained Glass Insurance: Once the photographic history and the stained glass appraisal is in place, the building and grounds committee is in position to carefully study the fine arts section of its church property insurance.

It is no disrespect to say that most church insurance agents have a limited understanding of stained glass values. How could they? There are no stained glass appraisal schools and the subtleties of artistic detail along with age are learned only with many years of stained glass study (not in the classrooms, but in church, after church, after church).

Therefore, without a professional appraisal, the cost to replicate your congregation's stained glass windows is decidedly different (possibly much more, possibly much less) than what is in your church insurance policy.

Since stained glass is usually the single most valuable art piece in the church building, and may also be the most vulnerable, it is essential to know its value and then subsequently to assure it is insured against partial or total loss. With that photographic record and a professional insurance appraisal, the insurance company will normally accept its validity and insure the stained glass accordingly. One can never be too careful with a congregation's rich, artistic heritage.

Exterior stained glass view of First United Methodist Church in downtown Gulfport, Mississippi. The unbreakable polycarbonate protective covering had been professionally installed and was able to survive without difficulty Hurricane Katrina.

Protective Covering: Since I have now inspected some two thousand sets of stained glass windows in the last two decades, there is one statement that can be made without equivocation, *protect your leaded stained glass windows!*

Protection is certainly a stewardship issue. Leaded stained glass windows deteriorate at a much more rapid rate without protection (need to be releaded every 60 years) vs. those with a protective covering (releaded at about 150 years). The difference a church has spent in patch-work restoration in the meantime is often ridiculous!

Important is protecting the church's art masterpieces from damage or possibly even destruction. If the stained glass is extremely valuable, it needs to be protected by a nearly unbreakable polycarbonate sheet (usually LEXAN XL made by General Electric). If your church has a LaFarge or Tiffany window, protect it with a polycarbonate.

If your windows are valuable and your parish is located on the Atlantic, Pacific, or Gulf coasts, or you worry about hail or vandalism, then apply a polycarbonate protective covering (by a stained glass company that specializes in protective covering, not a local company that makes "cute" transoms for residents of the local community).

Regrettably polycarbonates, even the improved versions, have not proven to stay aesthetically attractive for long periods of time. They begin to cloud (and sometimes yellow) in about 12-20 years when subjected to significant sunlight. Since it is expensive to install and polycarbonates become aesthetically unattractive so rapidly, many churches with lesser-valued windows have used glass as a protective covering alternative.

Glass as a protection is wise IF, the three above steps have been completed:

1)   a complete photographic inventory,
2)   a professional stained glass appraisal, and
3)   proper fine art insurance coverage.

A basic rule for protective covering should be used:

> *If a window could be easily replaced (which are at least 2/3rds of American stained glass church windows), then glass (or possibly acrylic) protective coverings may be considered; it's probably even wise.*

If a window is an older pictorial, would be difficult or impossible to replace, then a polycarbonate protective covering is required.

The extremely valuable pictorial stained glass in the sanctuary at First United Methodist Church in Gulfport, Mississippi, had been protected professionally using a polycarbonate. These windows were about the only ones (along with those at First Christian) to avoid damage. Many windows in the FUMC educational building had havoc wreaked upon them by Katrina. The church had taken a risk with these lesser windows, and fortunately they had their windows insured.

Stained glass is becoming increasingly valuable and often irreplaceable as the great stained glass studios and artists of the last two centuries age and disappear. Typically, it is the stained glass that represents by far the most valuable single items in the church building.

It is wise and good stewardship, therefore, to take the necessary steps to ensure your windows will continue to inspire future generations in the same manner those of past generations have witnessed and enjoyed.

Ford Brothers stained glass window at The Church of the
Holy Cross Episcopal, Paris, Texas

Chapter VI

THE TALE OF TWO CHURCH SNAILS

The 150-Year Plan

Throughout America's congregations there exists two different church snails. One, the fast snail, has a life expectancy from forty to sixty years. The slow snail will live to be about 150.

The fast snail lives in churches in which the stained glass is not given preventative maintenance on a regular 25-40 year basis and is not protected from weather, vandals, accidents and burglary. As such, the fast snail utilizes the great weight of the stained glass and the lack of bracing to slowly deteriorate. The fast snail is helped along by children playing ball nearby or from a tree falling during major storms. Great heat from the Sun contributes to the snail's speed.

After as brief a time as 40 years, the fast stained glass snail has managed to develop massive bulges in the stained glass and the church property committee often opts to completely relead the windows—to essentially take the vertical jig-saw puzzle apart, and rebuild it like new. Releading is like a complete overhaul of a motor—it fixes the problem, but maybe only a small part was missing. Releading is often massive overkill.

Why? It is essential to understand the basics. Stained glass is an extremely heavy vertical jig-saw puzzle made up of 1) *glass*, usually either stained or painted/fired, 2) *lead cames* with two channels for the glass to fit into, and 3) *cement* that secures the glass and the lead together. The glass will exist for many centuries or until broken, the lead came can last at least 150 years, but the cement starts caking immediately. The cement is probably the most critical element of long-term care. Under controlled situations, the lead should not be the interim concern.

The 150-Year Plan

Most churches that house slow snails know they are there. They never allow their snail to turn into a fast one. Instead, they work on a basic 150-year stained glass plan.

The new stained glass at Baylor Baptist Hospital, Plano (Texas) chapel was protected by glass set in a heavy-duty aluminum frame.

Protect New Windows

First, when the leaded stained glass is new, the property committee makes sure a protective covering is installed (between ½" and 3" away from the stained glass for good insulation). If the windows are extremely valuable and/or are in a vandal prone area, this protective covering should be General Electric's Lexan XL which is nearly unbreakable. Since new high quality pictorial stained glass is sometimes priced as much as $500 to $900 per square foot, this unbreakable quality in the protective covering is required. Unfortunately even the new, improved Lexan XL, discolors over the years and generally has an aesthetically pleasing look for no more than 20 years.

Therefore, most churches are installing ¼" glass as the protective covering. Although breakable, glass is still strong and takes away the psychological temptation for children to throw rocks at those little bulls-eyes in the stained glass. Most important, glass continues to look nice on the exterior of a church building.

The Thirty-year "Oil change"

Just like an automobile needs an oil change every 3,000 miles, so the slow church snail needs attention every 25-30 years. Several important preventative maintenance steps need to be taken.

First, the protective covering will be removed to allow access to the exterior of the stained glass. Second, a fresh application of cement is applied to the exterior of the window. This process brilliantly cleans the exterior of the window but more importantly both strengthens the windows and enlivens the old lead. Third, the window frame (if wooden) is scraped, primed and repainted. Finally new protective covering is installed, usually (and hopefully) in a perimeter aluminum frame.

It is during the 25-30 year oil change that additional work may be needed to keep your church snail slow. Some bulging may have occurred because of the window's great weight, tightness due to improper installation, or to insufficient bracing. The panels with bulges can be removed during the process, laid flat on a table, restored, braced, and reinstalled without ever leaving the church property. Broken pieces of stained glass can be replaced.

Plan to Reload in 2160 or so…

If the slow church snail has preventative maintenance every 30 years, the feared reload process can wait 150 years. Thus new leaded stained glass installed in 2010 would and frankly should not be releaded until 2160!!! Most of us will not need to worry about chairing that reload committee.

Finally, there is no question that stained glass is the most beautiful way to tell the biblical story through God's light. Stained glass has been used throughout history as God's first slide show to use pictures to present the Bible visually to the illiterate masses.

Today stained glass remains a precious inspiration tool for the local church but one that needs proper preventative maintenance and protection over the years. If planned, your church will have a slow snail in charge of your lead deterioration rather than that fast paced snail that will have you releading expensive stained glass in just a few decades.

First Baptist Church in Enid, Oklahoma

Chapter VII

HOW TO INSPECT
YOUR STAINED GLASS

Stained glass is simply a vertical jig-saw puzzle. As a result, stained glass, because it is quite heavy and is often left to exposure by weather, is subject to deterioration—snail paced to be sure—that is consistent. Left to deteriorate…it will and sometimes priceless pieces of carefully inspired and crafted artwork are destroyed by neglect.

Value of Stained Glass

Many leadership committees assume that because their forefathers paid $4,000 for the stained glass in 1898, the value is still relatively small. These could now have replacement values forty to one hundred times that amount. This, of course, does not mean that a congregation could take their windows out of the frame and expect to sell them for even a fraction of the cost—the religious nature of the glass and the unique shape of the overall window normally makes resale, even if desired, unrealistic. But let the windows deteriorate to the point where they literally fall out of the frame, and sticker shock will set in. Even on-site "restoration" and "preventive maintenance" is not inexpensive, but it is far less so than replicating a window.

Inspecting Stained Glass

Even simple stained glass designs are subject to degradation and must be inspected every decade or so to insure the continued "health" of the window for the inspiration of future generations of worshippers. So how does the minister or property chairperson know whether stained glass needs attention or not? Do a personal inspection tour. Here's what to look for:

Lead: If lead has been protected and given preventative maintenance over the years, *the lead cames should not need replacement for at least 150 years!* Many churches, on the basis of recommendations from stained glass companies—and fears of losing their windows by jittery lay people—have been known to relead every couple of decades.

Look directly at the lead (don't worry about anything else for the time being) and try to determine how often you can find breaks in the lead itself. Multiple breaks through-out a window means releading is probably going to be essential. However, this should be occurring only in windows one hundred or more years old or ones that have not had a protective covering (glass or plastic) since they were new. When the windows reach 150 years, the window is ready to relead regardless, although preventive maintenance can often get another 30 or more years of life.

The Bulge: A bulge can threaten a stained glass panel more than anything else. This bulging or buckling effect may extend inward or outward as much as 3" and eventually (when left unattended) the stained glass will simply fall out of the frame. This is caused by the great weight of the stained glass, deterioration from weather, and poor bracing.

Bulge: This Franz Meyer window (Munich & London) at St. Mark's Episcopal Church, Cheyenne, Wyoming is bulging so badly the lead (see arrow) is separating. Soon (within five to ten years) the bulged area will buckle and the panel will slowly collapse breaking numerous pieces of painted/fired glass in the process.

Get close to the window from the interior and look upward at the window. Try to determine if the stained glass is vertically flat or not, or has one or several locations throughout the window that are forming a rounded curve (or folding effect) either inward or outward. Simply focus on each panel looking for bulges, then move to the next panel, and so on. If the windows are vertical, that's good. If you see bulges of at least 1" from vertical, the deterioration process is in motion already to eventually lose the windows.

Braces: Steel braces (usually the width/length of the stained glass panel) are used to secure the stained glass panel of lead came, glass, and cement and keep it vertical. These braces can be both vertical and horizontal, and some-times at an angle.

Most modern braces are rectangular, while 100-year plus windows often have rounded braces tightened at the joints by wire. They are soldered at the lead joint areas (or wired tight) and then secured at both ends into the window frame. Bulges do not commence in areas of the stained glass panels where bracing has been properly placed and remain tightly secured.

First Baptist Church in Enid, Oklahoma

From the interior of the stained glass window, take hold of each brace to determine if you can get movement. No movement is good. Check both ends of the brace to see if it is firmly attached to the frame. Also determine if the original solder is holding at the lead joints crossed by the brace. Loosened braces, prior to a bulge developing, can be corrected relatively easily but must be addressed or other problems will begin to occur.

Glass: There are two forms of what is generically called stained glass. Some glass is originally manufactured in sheets with a color and variety of colors built-in. That glass is referred to here as *stained glass*. Other glass is (often clear glass) painted one layer at a time by an artist, and then fired to a heat level that allows the paint to be absorbed into the glass. This process, referred to here as *painted/fired glass*, is repeated until the desired appearance is achieved. Small pieces of both stained glass and/or painted/fired glass are then placed into a larger artistic panel to fabricate (via the lead came, cement, and steel braces).

Obviously, glass can be broken and poorly painted/fired glass can fade. Nothing bothers a person sitting in the pew trying to listen to a dull sermon more than seeing a broken piece of glass letting streams of light pour through. A close rival for irritation is a badly mismatched repair where now a green piece of glass is located where a brown piece was originally.

This old faded medallion at First United Methodist, Gulfport, Mississippi has been shattered during Hurricane Katrina. It can be copied, painted, and fired to either look like new or have built in fade.

Look at each individual piece of glass to see if you can spot cracks, breaks, bullet holes, and badly mismatched glass. Caution: stained glass is very hard to match, even by those who say the match will be perfect, so my recommendation is to leave as many pieces as possible with only one crack or two minor ones (as you will be less pleased with a mismatch). Those with multiple cracks easily visible from the pew need attention.

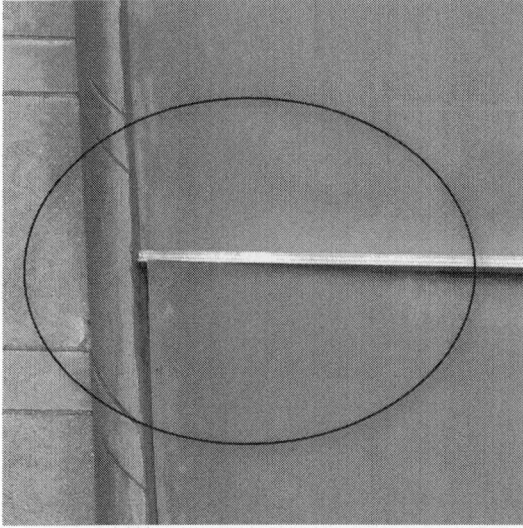

This protective covering was set stone-to-stone and sealed at the edges with silicone some 25 years ago. Now pulled away, water is seeping inside and causing damage to the wood, metal, and stained glass.

Cement: Normally, the first stained glass element to deteriorate is the cement between the lead came and the glass. The cement should be "recemented" every twenty-five years or so. The recementing process is a simple and old fashioned one of applying a cementing compound to the exterior (often with a simple paint brush!) and then rubbing it off with a rag or brush, leaving the new cement to intermingle with the old cement. The result is a restrengthened, somewhat water and air tight joint, and a brilliantly clean exterior window. Recementing is the single most important preventative maintenance step for the continued healthy life of your stained glass!

While standing on the interior side of the stained glass, press firmly on the center of a lead joint near the middle of a stained glass panel. If you get movement and/or hear a caking sound, recementing is needed.

Protective Covering: When most Roman Catholic churches were built in the 1890-1917 era, the new stained glass was automatically protected with a glass outer coating. Much of this original glass still exists and in many instances, the interior stained glass (often priceless in its biblical stories and art) remains substantially intact with few problems. Conversely most protestant churches built during those same eras were not originally protected, and those churches have been paying for that choice for decades. Bulges, bullet holes, vandalism, hail, and

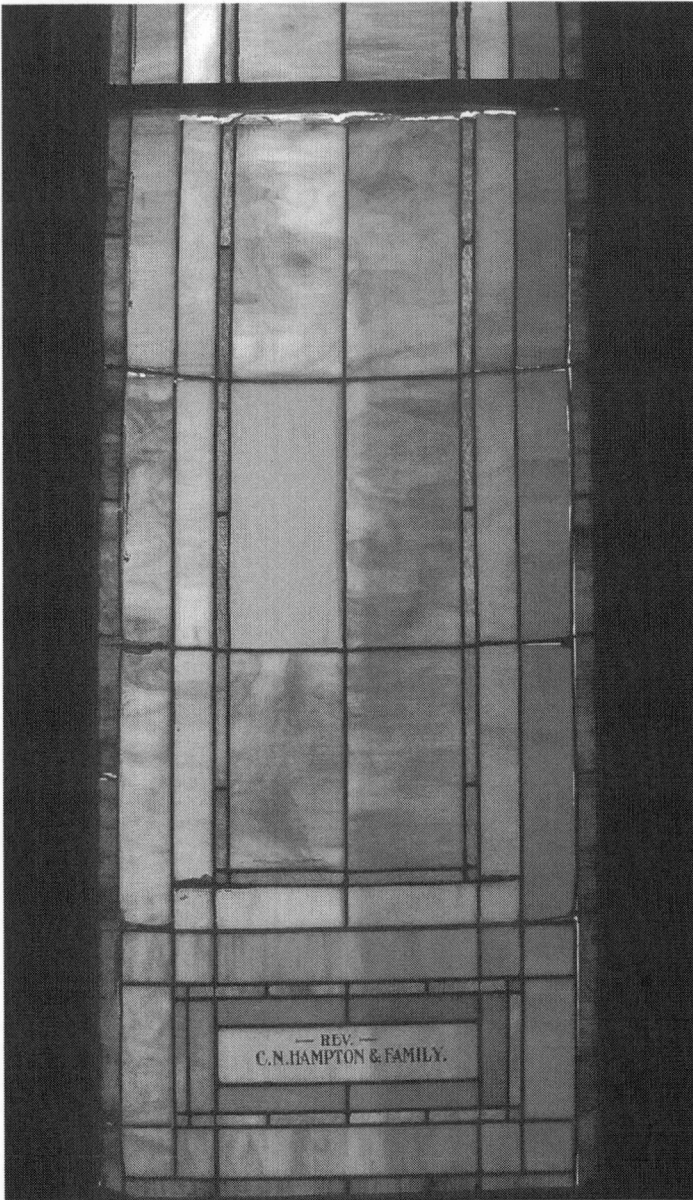

This St. Paul Baptist Church, Paris, Texas panel is in the final stages of collapse. It requires releading…there is no other choice. This picture indicates the difficulty of matching stained glass. In this case, the church will be wise to sacrifice one of its windows to provide matching stained glass for the others. The one that is scavenged is then recreated with new stained glass with the closest possible match.

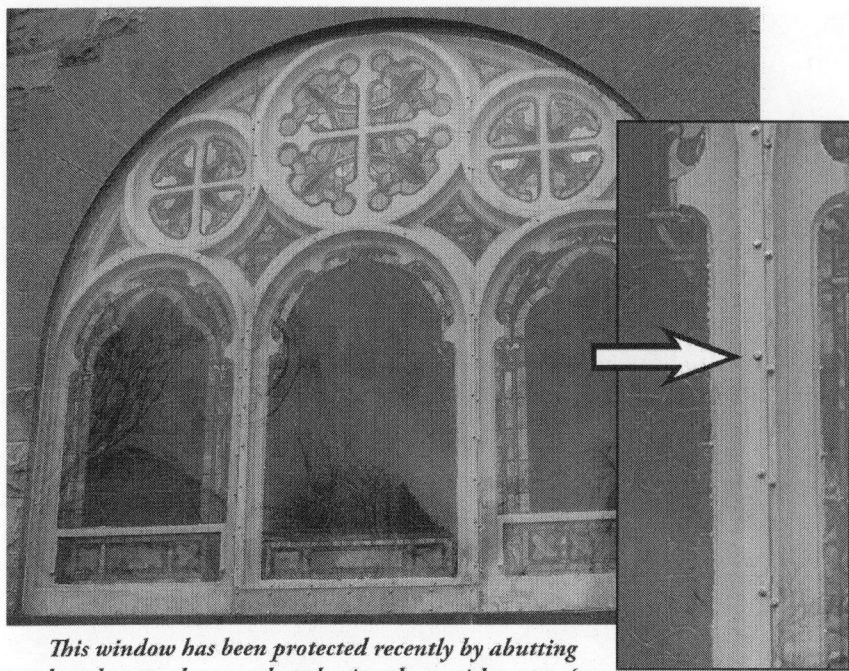

This window has been protected recently by abutting polycarbonate sheets and anchoring them with screws (see arrow) to the wood stained glass frames. Water, dust, and insects will all soon infiltrate the protective cover causing the exterior stained glass appearance to be unacceptable within only a few years, while offering only modest protection. More harm was done than good.

robbery have each played havoc. Although it is not the perfect answer, most deterioration problems and outside hazards are eliminated when protective covering is in place sheltering the stained glass from day-to-day weather, severe storms, vandalism, and robbery.

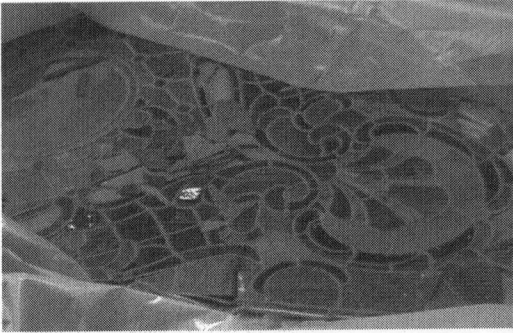

When Hurricane Rita ripped into the Tyrell Historical Library, Beaumont, Texas, this panel was blown onto the library floor. Remarkably, the panel sustained only about 20 broken pieces but the medallion was destroyed. The damage was sufficient enough to require a complete panel relead, in addition to the replacement of the broken glass and an expert recreation of the painted/fired medallion. It needed to be releaded "using its sister panel as the model."

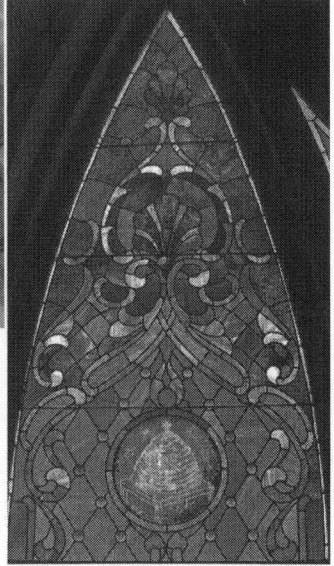

When inspecting the protective covering look for four things.

First, is the protective covering now "ugly" and detracting from the overall appearance of the church campus?

Second, are there pieces broken?

Third, is the window still "sealed" or is water causing rot and condensation problems?

Finally, if your church has wood rather than stone frames, inspect the paint and caulk between the stained glass and the protective covering to determine its condition.

After the Inspection

If you have found bulges, soft cement, broken glass, and ugly protective covering, then contact professionals (three different ones) for their suggestions and costs. If you are one of about seventy-five percent of churches today that have their windows well maintained, then rest assured this portion of your church's heritage and ministry has been inspected and is not a concern.

University Baptist Church in Ft. Worth, Texas

Chapter VIII

THE LEVELS OF
STAINED GLASS RESTORATION

As a stained glass consultant for two decades, I have become conscious of how unaware property committees are about their congregation's leaded stained glass. I'm not referring here to the stained glass itself.

Indeed, if the church has special windows, all the people have a tremendous pride in them, and congregants' carry knowledge about them to talk informatively to visitors.

> *"Our windows on the north side tell different stories of the Old Testament—that's Moses with the Ten Commandments there."* Then they turn to the other side with *"and the south side tells the story of Jesus. It starts with our beautiful Nativity window on the right and ends with the Ascension into Heaven. I just love them. Aren't they lovely?"*

Most people do not know the leaded stained glass is in "trouble" just from the long-term deterioration that comes with simple aging. However, when they do see a window beginning to bulge, some property committee members will talk about it for years, and do nothing. Others panic and want to have all the windows releaded immediately. Both approaches are wrong.

Dealing with stained glass systematically is critical; because stained glass does have needs…when and how those windows are addressed determines their long-term health, plus the potentially hefty costs to repair/restore problems.

My experience indicates stained glass has five different levels—degrees—of restoration needs. When the property committee becomes aware of its stained glass condition, it is wise to identify what level of restoration is required to solve the problems.

Restoration Level #1: The Stained Glass Oil Change

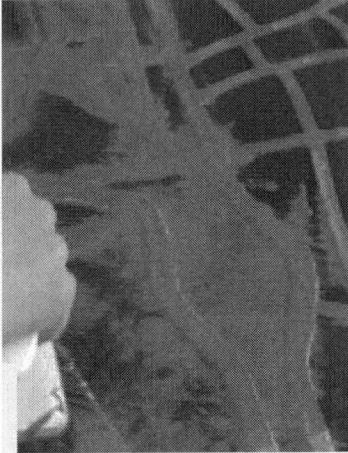

Recementing: The cement (holding the lead came and the stained glass together) begins to cake after several decades. One of the most important stained glass preventive steps is the replenishment of cement. A cementing compound is brushed over each square inch of the stained glass surface, then buffed off, leaving the old cement enlivened and the exterior stained glass brilliantly clean.

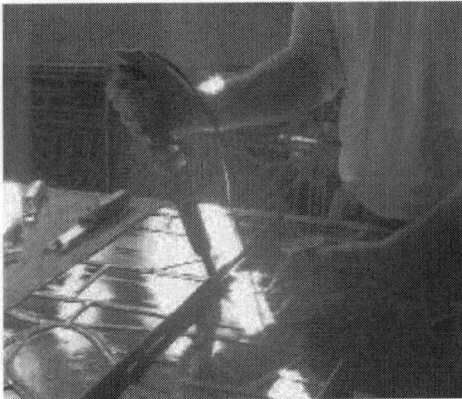

Steel Braces: Once a panel is removed and a bulge flattened by master artisans, vertical and/or horizontal steel braces are soldered to the lead to strengthen the panel against future bulging.

All leaded stained glass is essentially made the same way and with only three basic items: the cut stained glass, the lead came which has channels for the glass to fit, and cement to hold the glass and the came together. Simple.

Of the three, the glass will last the longest, if it is not broken. The lead came, it seems, can easily last for 150 years if it has been fortunate to have had protective covering during the bulk of those years. But the poor, poor cement often has a relatively short life and needs to be replenished every 15-30 years (again depending on whether the windows have protective covering).

Thus, the wise congregation will build in a process to have its windows recemented every 15 years (if unprotected) and each 25-30 (if protected).

The process of recementing is simple. A liquid cementing compound is applied to the exterior of the leaded stained glass, then rubbed in manually so the new liquid cement is intermingled with the old. Once the new/old cement dries, the window is nearly back to new—strong and clean and ready to let the inspiration of its message continue.

Restoration Level #2: Simple Jig Saw Puzzle Repairs

The creators of most art objects are justifiably proud of their "masterpieces." Not surprisingly, the stained glass field is filled with outstanding artisans who take great joy in their window telling a story through glass. Despite their knowledge that stained glass panels bulge, steel braces are often limited because their resulting lines and shadows detract from the message and aesthetics of the art. Trouble!!!

A stained glass panel is extremely heavy, and since it is, in essence, a vertical jig-saw puzzle, it will start to sag over the years…unless it is properly braced.

Other early problems develop. Often pieces of stained glass are broken (there's that need to keep the windows protected again!), or possibly the caulking begins to fail.

This calls for simple general repair. Horizontal steel braces can be added while the stained glass panel is still in place. Caulking can be replaced and the window frames repainted, along with recementing. Broken pieces of glass can be individually installed in place.

If some of the windows have begun to sag just a bit, they too can be adjusted while in place, then—in that very area—a steel brace needs to be installed—or that sag will come back in a few years and develop into a bulge in 25 years. Artisans will even add new braces to areas that are "vulnerable to bulging," important long-term preventive maintenance.

Restoration Level # 3: On-Site Bulge Repair

Regrettably, the stained glass consultant is often not called to evaluate problems until this level. If matters have been left dormant until this stage, the congregation will never quite get their windows back to "normal." The broken pieces of glass will not be 100% matched and the lead will forever show faint but definite signs of decay.

A quick survey by a trained eye will find small-to-large bulges in a number of the stained glass panels. If caught soon enough, an on-site master artisan can correct the bulges in-place and add the necessary braces. The wise property committee will use this opportunity to recement, repaint, and recaulk.

Restoration Level #4: Restoration

If the church waits to bring in the consultant this long, they will be in for some significant bad news…both about their windows and the exorbitant costs it will take to save them.

Removing Stained Glass: When stained glass needs significant restoration (such as this window from University Baptist Church, Fort Worth), each panel is removed from its frame then laid on a work table either at the church itself or is transferred to the stained glass studio for restoration.

In this situation, the windows are usually found with serious, possibly critical bulges in which the windows sag as much as 3" to 4" from their original form, braces have been loosened and are no longer attached to the panel, and some of the stained glass has been broken from the pressure and even come partially or totally out of their lead came channel.

When the windows have reached this point, only two remedies remain. First, the building and grounds committee can start over and have the windows releaded. Since leaded stained glass with proper preventive maintenance (the stained glass oil changes, etc.) should last at least 150 years between releadings, to do so in some 50 to 85 years, as often happens, is a stewardship travesty.

Second, if the stained glass still has strong lead, as it often does even while bulging, the window can be "restored". This restoration can take place either at the church (on a special work table set up by an on-site restoration crew), or removed to the stained glass studio for complete attention.

In both cases, a stained glass panel will quickly lose its bulge when laid flat, especially after some chemicals and/or heat is applied. When a panel is "restored," it receives a careful cementing process on both sides of the panel and is rebraced. When reinstalled, it's not quite as good as new, but close.

Restoration Level #5: Relead

If your church's windows are 150 years old, as many on America's east coast are, or if the windows have not been protected over the years, or if they have been neglected to such a degree that the lead is splitting, glass is pulling out of the cames, and broken pieces abound, then releading is probably the best or only course. This process is done at the stained glass studio.

Releading is simple. The stained glass jig saw puzzle is disassembled; then reassembled with new lead and cement. In the process, broken or mismatched glass is replaced and new braces are attached (often at the wrong places).

This must be made clear—Restoration Level #5: Releading is a superior process to any of the other restoration degrees. There are many situations when it is the only course for the property committee to consider.

Caution: Often when a window is taken into a studio to be "releaded," it has actually only been "restored" at "relead" prices. Carefully study the lead when it is returned to learn if the church has been "had," or not.

Releading is also much more expensive and the prices are increasing daily. Be aware that stained glass studios prefer to do the work at their studios—that's noble and understandable—but prices should be less rather than greater under the circumstances. They never are.

Many studios do not have the expertise to do on-site work—most make their living creating new stained glass so when repair work on old windows is required, the panels are approached in the same manner: the window is disassembled, and then they relead the various pieces until the panel is "new" again. They have repaired the window by starting over.

If your church windows have not been planned and cared with a master 150-year plan, then work with your stained glass company to conduct the restoration at the same level as its problems merit.

If you do, God's light will continue to shine through to worshipers for generations to come.

Cathedral of St. Helena in Helena, Montana

Chapter IX

PROTECTING YOUR STAINED GLASS HERITAGE ·

If you are ever in Helena, Montana, there is something that you must see. I am not referring to the state capital building or the Missouri River that was followed by Lewis and Clark 200 years ago on their way to the Bitterroot Mountains and on to the Pacific Ocean. Rather, I am suggesting you experience the Cathedral of St. Helena, an absolutely magnificent church edifice located in a region of the country where a building of this magnitude would never be anticipated. But there it is towering over Helena.

This grand cathedral is filled with over seventy large yet intricately painted/fired leaded stained glass windows created by the F. X. Zettler Co. (The Royal Bavarian Art Institute) of Munich, Germany near the beginning of the last century...thus the windows have offered a century of magnificent inspiration. In all, the Cathedral of St. Helena has 13,000 square feet of stained glass...absolutely a staggering amount, since most large churches seldom have more than 3,000 square feet!!!

Several years ago, cathedral officials were shocked to find stained glass pieces falling to the ground. A bulge had slowly developed in one of the stained glass panels and went unnoticed as it increasingly worsened until eventually breaking because of deterioration, heat, and its own great weight. It simply, ever so slowly, fell down. The officials immediately went about finding someone to repair the damage.

Recently, I had the opportunity to view this great cathedral as light was pouring into the nave. I had been asked to conduct an inspection of the remaining stained glass, but simply couldn't for several moments as I was so overwhelmed by the message I was receiving from the great biblical artwork.

I watched as others entered to see this great nave. Although the cathedral is filled with other great pieces of art, these other visitors too were drawn to the scriptures that were being shown to them visually through a release of brilliant hues. It was a feast of scripture, light and color.

Finally, I gained my composure and started inspecting window-by-window (in this case the rows of windows on top of each other), looking for further damage. These windows had NEVER been repaired (except for that one panel that had bulged). I expected hundreds of additional bulges. To my utter amazement, there were none...in fact there was not even a broken or cracked piece of painted/fired glass. *How could that possibly be?*

The answer was discovered on the exterior of the window frame. Back 100 years ago, clear glass was intricately cut and installed on the exterior of the stained glass tracery about 1/4" inch from the stained glass, essentially protecting the stained glass from accidents, weather, vandalism and burglary. That doesn't mean that the stained glass isn't in a slow process of deterioration, it is simply EXTREMELY slow.

The Catholics vs. the Protestants

It is not my intent here to start a new battle between the catholics and the protestants, nor to even discuss the football battles between Notre Dame and Southern Methodist. Rather, I can say from the inspection of so many thousands of stained glass windows that Roman Catholic windows not only are the highest artistic quality (along with Episcopalian) on average, they are normally in the best condition. The reason is simple: almost every catholic church automatically used a protective glass covering for their stained glass from the very moment the original stained glass was installed; the protestant churches did not.

Therefore, since the 1950s, an entire industry of stained glass restoration specialists have mostly been working on protestant windows. It started first in the northern states where the weather was playing the most havoc on unprotected stained glass. Then by the 1980s the sun had done its job on the unsuspecting southern churches. In other words, there have been many more meetings of the Board of Trustees in protestant churches concerning stained glass during the last half century than parish councils in their catholic counterparts. The lesson should be very plain to everyone: *PROTECT YOUR LEADED STAINED GLASS WINDOWS!!!*

Glass vs. Plastic Coverings

During the 1970s churches began using a polycarbonate (the most commonly used was Lexan produced by General Electric) protective covering that was nearly unbreakable for their windows. It became immensely popular, but began to come under disfavor just years later when the polycarbonate discolored and collected dust. Even the new advanced polycarbonates with UV ray protection will last aesthetically attractive no more than twenty years.

Thus, churches in recent years have returned to what the catholics have done for more than a century—use glass as a protective covering. And even with a number of glass options available, most are viewing basic business quality glass (float) as the most sensible, or the protection that safety glass provides for the more valuable stained glass.

Using our lessons from the past as a guide, the polycarbonate should be used when the stained glass is extremely valuable and cannot be replaced (such as a Tiffany and LaFarge or early day windows from studios like Lamb, Connick, or Jacoby), and/or when the windows are in high-prone vandalism areas. In all other cases, because of the long-term aesthetic benefits, glass is re-emerging as the preferred protective covering of choice.

New protective covering set with a perimeter frame by Stained Glass by Shenandoah at St. Paul United Methodist Church in Louisville, Kentucky

Note: In between glass and the polycarbonate is a third and much less used option: acrylic. Acrylic is stronger than glass but not as strong against impact as the polycarbonate. Acrylic will discolor, but at a rate much slower than the polycarbonate (clear glass discolors at an extremely slow rate).

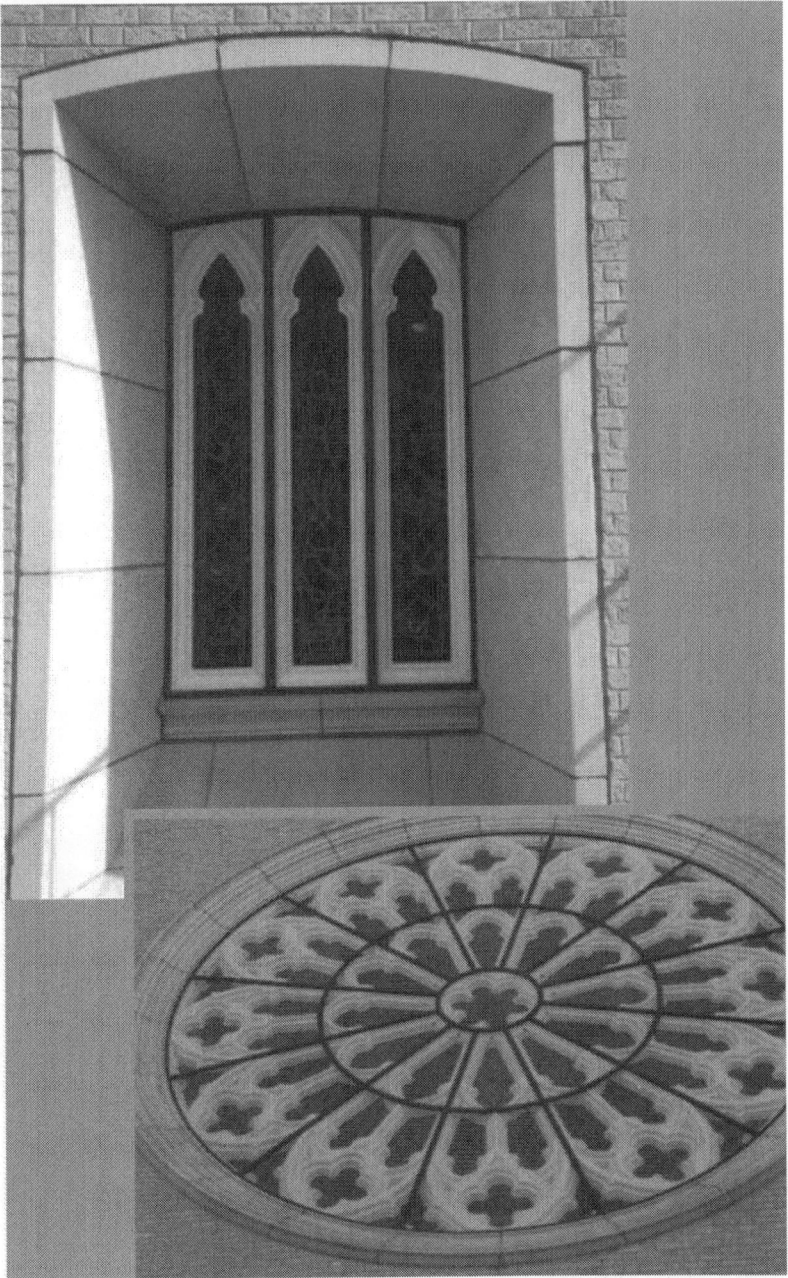

New protective covering with perimeter frame
at Broadway Baptist Church in Ft. Worth, Texas

The church property committee should carefully weigh this decision or its counterpart committee twenty years later will also have it on the agenda. A quick survey of protective covering options is warranted.

3/16" LEXAN XL is the protective coating churches have had installed on stained glass since the 1960s. It is unbreakable (almost) and normally remains aesthetically pleasing for about 20 years. The original LEXAN discolored in about six years. The new advanced product, with a U/V protective coating, is much improved, but being a plastic, will get cloudy and dusty at some point. Protected windows directly facing the sun start clouding within ten years and are unattractive at about seventeen.

¼" LEXAN XL is obviously thicker than 3/16" LEXAN and therefore will remain more firm over the years. It will be only slightly more effective at protection, but since most of the windows can be installed with larger pieces of protective covering, the ¼" LEXAN might look better long-term.

Before   *After*

These before and after photos of a window at St. Mary's Episcopal Church in Eldorado, Arkansas, illustrate the stark contrast from old cloudy polycarbonate protective coverings with a new one. This window is set stone-to-stone. In neither case was a perimeter frame used, which will become a problem in about 25 years.

¼" Float Glass is used in most business settings and is gaining popularity with churches because it will remain attractive for a long time (if not broken). Should the float glass protective covering be broken, and

Before   *After*

Before and after photos of a window at First Christian Church, Pendleton, Oregon.

*These windows at First Presbyterian Church, Bozeman, Montana
are examples of the protective covering being set in the exterior wooden
frame and tracery. While this approach is among the most attractive settings,
the exterior frames will need repainting every five years or so, plus the millwork
is exposed to the elements leading to the strong possibility of long-term rot.*

some of your stained glass is also broken, most of the shattered pieces can be matched nearly to perfection. The advantage of float glass is that it will continue to look nice for many years, and will be removed possibly only because repair will be needed on the stained glass or the exterior frame (in which it was set) is needing repainting or beginning to deteriorate (this is probably 30 years down the road).

¼" **Safety Glass** provides the benefits of the long-term appearance of glass, but also protects the stained glass to the extremely heavy blow (that might break ¼" float glass). The safety glass will break as well, but it will not shatter. The reason is that it is made with 1/8" glass, then plastic, then another 1/8" glass layer. Thus, if broken, the plastic layer holds together, usually allowing the precious stained glass underneath to avoid breakage.

Quality installed protective covering along with careful preventative maintenance is the best insurance that releading can indeed be delayed for those many decades. The beautiful stained glass at the Cathedral of St. Helena is ample proof of what protective covering means to the prolonged healthy life of leaded stained glass.

St. Michael's Catholic Church in Biloxi, Mississippi following Hurricane Katrina

Chapter X

PROTECTING STAINED GLASS AGAINST DISASTERS

The stories were incredible. Two priests were inside the nave of Catholic Cathedral of the Nativity of the Blessed Virgin Mary in Biloxi when Hurricane Katrina hit the Gulf Coast. The nave walls began to heave. A door was opened, and suddenly a small transom stained glass window was sucked from its frame. Because the stained glass had a protective covering, the priceless stained glass windows, at least those that remained, were badly damaged but saved.

No one was at St. Michael's Catholic Church located on the ultimate southeast point on Biloxi's coast. It is a good thing, as no one would have survived. Not only was the church dramatically impacted by hurricane level 5 force winds, but a water surge 130" high simply waltzed through the chapel and nave taking glass protective covering, multiple tall stained glass panels, the altar, pews, and everything else that caught its fancy.

Across the street, a floating gambling casino was lifted from its moorings and was found sitting in the church's yard the next morning. To the unobservant, it appeared as a normal but slightly damaged office building…it was now only a worthless boat located at the wrong place.

My job was to recommend what should be done with the forty windows that were now standing empty in the lower 130" of the frame. Our eventual plan called for the chapel stained glass to be replicated.

A totally different approach was used for the nave. We wanted something strong, but less expensive than the stained glass that had been destroyed. The thinking: if St. Michael's was hit by one hurricane level 5, another may come along someday. Therefore, rather than replacing the extremely valuable stained glass, the approach was to place 50% tinted glass in a bronze-toned aluminum double-track frame. The exterior track would have ¼" LEXAN XL, a nearly unbreakable polycarbonate protective covering.

Each of these windows would have a project-in ventilator. If another Katrina had its eye focused on Biloxi, then all of the ventilators would be left wide open to take the pressure off the building when the storm surge is at its greatest.

This leads the discussion to a very important series of questions and dilemmas. What lessons did we learn from this disaster? When do we protect for massive breakage or do we take risks and hope for long-term beauty?

It depends, mostly, on whether it is more important for your church to protect valuable windows (without any fear of outside breakage) or, to have long term outside beauty with your protective covering.

That said, what about churches worried about the impact of hurricanes, tornados or huge pieces of hail? What about vandalism or robbery? What if the church has priceless pieces of Tiffany glass or other magnificent pieces of stained glass art?

St. Michael's Catholic Church in Biloxi had floor to ceiling stained glass in both the chapel and the nave. The Hurricane Katrina storm surge took all stained glass below the 130" mark.

St. Peter's by the Sea Episcopal Church, Gulfport was overwhelmed by Hurricane Katrina's storm surge that effectively obliterated the nave's lower level.

Then, the question is answered quickly. Install as the protective covering a poly-carbonate (normally 3/16" Clear LEXAN XL) for maximum protection. Do so, however, knowing that this protection will stay attractive a maximum of 25 years and possibly only 10 years when directly facing the sun.

What if the church is not on the front line of potential hurricanes like Biloxi, Mississippi? What if the windows are not priceless, but can easily be replaced?

This leads to other answers. Many churches that are no longer worried about van-dalism, major storms, and know their windows to be less than priceless, are now using glass as their protective coverings, mostly the float glass variety. They prefer the long-term aesthetics glass promises, and are willing to take some risk of break-age over the years. Some churches, with valuable stained glass, choose to protect their windows from breakage using ¼" safety glass.

Churches facing the constant threat of hurricanes have little option. They need to use an unbreakable polycarbonate to protect their windows. Churches elsewhere have more options, and the decision should be based on the value of the stained glass being protected, and how long it will be before the protective covering is replaced.

Each protective covering has its advantages and corresponding disadvantages. Know them and match these to your church windows in making the wise protective covering choice for your congregation.

First Baptist Church in Enid, Oklahoma

Chapter XI

PICKING STAINED GLASS

Comparing Stained Glass Apples and Oranges

Imagine you are a church with stained glass needs and you read in a newspaper of a unique orchard, one with stained glass trees. Trees there are all in neat little rows, all properly sprayed and fertilized, and the grounds are immaculately tilled. The advertisement claims there are four varieties of stained glass trees and invites you, the church public, to come pick "all you want."

Out of curiosity, you feel an overwhelming need to see this one-of-a-kind orchard. Deciding to take your minister and several lay leaders with you in the church van, your little group arrives at the entrance of the stained glass orchard, there to be greeted by Mr. Green, the foreman.

After some coffee, he asks you what you want to see. *"I've never seen a stained glass orchard,"* you say, *"so I don't even know what to expect or what to ask."* With that the tour begins.

Riding in an orchard cart, your group first sees a huge number, possibly as many as 2000, stained glass *PLUM* trees. Mr. Green explains:

> *The stained glass Plum is the most common variety. In fact, you will find at least one in nearly every town in America. They are primarily good for individual homes, and occasionally for the local church. Some plums are tastier than others, meaning some designs are quality while others are quite common. In addition, a stained glass plum is not always built properly, so it may not last as long as other stained glass fruits.*

The cart turned a corner to reveal a couple rows of stained glass *ORANGE* trees. Here Mr. Green comments:

> *These trees are mostly members of the Stained Glass Association of America and their fruits are not only the best tasting in the orchard, but the most expensive. Stained glass Orange trees total only about 60 in the whole country but have some of the finest artists and crafts people tending to their care. If you want a unique masterpiece in your church, you want an Orange.*

Over in the far Southeast corner of the orchard sat a few large stained glass *PEAR* trees. After halting the cart, Mr. Green tells your group these trees are rare, but are special in their taste. He points to the tallest tree:

> *Look carefully at the pears on that one there, some of them are exactly the same size, color, and shape. If you want some pears, simply pick the shape you want, tell the lady in charge how many you want, and a perfect set can be sent to your church in a few months. If you don't care if your pears look like those of the church down the road, these are not only attractive, but economical.*

Finally, Mr. Green points out the single row of stained glass *APPLE* trees. Some were tall with bright red apples, while others were small and not well groomed. He explains:

> *Stained glass apples are shipped around the country whenever a church has repair or protective covering needs. You don't go to an apple company when you want something new, but only later when you want to preserve what you have. Like any stained glass tree in the orchard, you must compare apples-to-apples, because there is a vast difference in quality and philosophy.*

Our little group was finally back to the orchard showroom. It was then that our church treasurer Suzy Wright asked Mr. Green: *So how do we choose the stained glass tree for our congregation?*

> *Ms. Wright, each and every one of these trees might be valuable for you. Let's look carefully at each one, to determine what best suits your needs.*
>
> *If you are a small church and want to install just a few stained glass windows, you might want to look at the stained glass PLUM. Because the stained glass plum tree is a local one, you can be involved with the process from design to installation, and normally the cost is relatively nominal.*

However, the design and fabrication quality varies dramatically. I strongly recommend you look at some of the other plum trees in the region before choosing. Remember, these plum trees do business with residences far more than churches, and you might be their largest client ever. Proceed with caution!

If you are a church in which the biblical message seen through God's light is of importance, and money is not an over-riding factor, then the stained glass **ORANGE** *should be strongly considered. Usually, the resulting stained glass is a 'masterpiece' that has been thoughtfully designed and created.*

Stained glass and money?—please know that no item in the life of the church, with the possible exception of a pipe organ, is as valuable for fund raising. Show your congregation a design that is biblically illuminating and creative, and the money is almost always available to finish the product. I've found the finer the stained glass vision, the greater the gifts to pay for it. Dream and it will happen.

If you need a large number of windows and your budget is a concern, the stained glass **PEAR** *tree is an option. The pear is often considered the 'catalog' fruit, because you can pick from a number of already created designs, biblical scenes and symbols. Since these pears are made in great quantity, the cost differential from oranges is significant."*

Finally there is the stained glass **APPLE**. *These are delivered on-site to the church when the original stained glass fruit is in need of repair or protective covering. If you have current stained glass windows needing repair, use an apple. Every other kind, the plum, the orange, and the pear, will want to completely relead (or at least restore at the studio) your window, which is extremely expensive.*

A stained glass apple will come to your church every 25 to 30 years to provide preventive maintenance (reducing bulges, adding steel braces, replacing cracked glass, and recementing the lead cames). If you use an apple every 25 or so years and keep your windows protected from the weather, vandals, and accidents, you will not need to relead your stained glass but every 150 years or so. The apple is your best source of restoration, protection, and insulation stewardship.

I know you'll want to discuss these among yourselves. We've created this little table to assist you with the strengths and weaknesses of each so you can truly compare stained glass fruits, apple-to-apple or apples and oranges."

Stained Glass Fruit Comparison Table

Fruit	New Windows	Restoration/Protection	Quality	Costs
Plum	Small Churches only.	Restoration by relead Poor protection technology	Low to medium	Low to medium
Orange	Large, liturgical, artistic churches	Restoration by relead Average protection technology	Medium to high	Medium to high
Pear	Similar design throughout	Restoration by relead Average protection technology	Medium	Low to medium
Apple	No	On-site repair, restoration Protection, and insulation Potentially high protection technology	Low to high	Low compared to relead

As your group is leaving, Mr. Green suggests that you check the Stained Glass Association in America website and that you look at several churches that have gone through similar needs assessment in your region to find out what stained glass fruit companies they used. As the group departed the stained glass orchard, he shouted:

Know your stained glass needs, and pick your stained glass from the right tree.

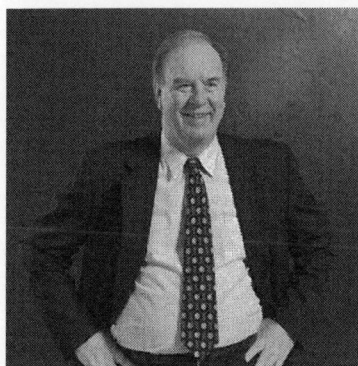

Dr. Gary M. Gray, FCBA

Dr. Gary M. Gray, stained glass consultant, has inspected and appraised stained glass in some two thousand churches and synagogues. He has conducted stained glass work in every state (among the "lower 48"), and is the author of eleven books and the former editor of two national Christian magazines. He holds graduate degrees from Phillips University, Southern Methodist University, and Notre Dame University, an American University Professional Certificate in Church Management, and a D. Ed. from Oklahoma State University.

Early in his career, Dr. Gray was the Executive Director of the National Institute on Church Management where he taught and consulted with thousands of ministers, church administrators, and military chapel administrators the concept of mission oriented management. The NICM was sanctioned by the National Association of Church Business Administration. Writing along with his brother, Dr. Robert N. Gray, the five-volume *Managing the Church* series served as pioneer volumes in this new and evolving profession. In 1996, Dr. Gray was named to the Church Management Hall of Fame.

Concurrent with his stained glass consultation, Dr. Gray has developed into a historian, writer, and actor renowned for his brilliant and historically accurate portrayals of seven of America's greatest citizens: Presidents Washington, Jefferson, A. Johnson, Garfield, T. Roosevelt and FDR, plus General of the Army, Douglas MacArthur. These portrayals were all gathered together in his recent book *Mr. Presidents: Voices of Freedom, Equality and Dignity*. See MrPresidents.com for details.

Dr. Gray may be contacted at 800-821-9595 or gary.gray@sbcglobal.net.

978-0-595-40374-5
0-595-40374-3

Made in the USA
Lexington, KY
22 January 2015